I0191425

Collection Of Poems

Through my mind

L. Chandrasekhar

/ BookLeaf
Publishing

India | USA | UK

Made with ❤ on the BookLeaf Publishing Platform
www.bookleafpub.in
www.bookleafpub.com

Dedication

I dedicate this small book of poetry to my kith and kin who inspired me to bring out this book.

Preface

It is a challenge and a cherished moment for all the
authors who took part on this esteemed platform who
has created the process of publishing our books from the
beginning to the final stage of printing.

It is a great opportunity of testimony for a poet to
endorse the caliber of poetry which motivates him in the
years to come by boosting their confidence.

I am very thankful to the editor and the whole team who
had put in efforts throughout the process of bringing out
this book so elegant and efficiently.

Acknowledgements

 My heartfelt gratitude to the entire team of Book Leaf
Publishers which made me possible to complete the
work in an organised manner
My sincere thanks to the editors, designers, publishers
etc., for their professional support .

Thank you all.

1. Rain Walk

Whilst the lurking sunshine
Invokes speculation of rain
Amid of towers I am gazing
Dark clouds are hovering
As I walk down the street
Sense the sweet smell of the gentle breeze.
Abruptly unison of the clouds
An appealing of pleasant sounds
As the rain in drizzling phase
People cheered to a change of grace
Long awaited for joyous moment
After scorching sun's heat and dust
When the droplets enrich shining of leaves.
Melody rhythms on metallic sheets
In an aura of wind like feast
As the clouds discolours from greyish dark
Gently flying cherished lark.
As drizzle ceased which designed shiny roads Before
dusk falls, the sun appeared
In its usual colour to red
After long lurking behind the cloud.

2. Verses of Universe

The era of primitive culture
Human has a peculiar nature
Staring glittering celestial bodies
Since the dawn of literature
Intensified his yearnings
The prudence dominated by curiosity
Concurrently led to creativity.

Man perceived to watch the skies
Beauteous star gazing nights
The wisdom of human race
Known after immense progress .
Route cause of the poetry
Has sown the seed of beauty of infinity
The sun, moon, planets, stars praised in divinity.

Poetries captivated image of the mankind
All the communities of globe inspired
Laid the foundation of hunger
To invent varied flights to reach farther .
Poet defined the beauty of cosmos
With his precious verses of horizons
So poet is the main scholar
Who awaken other professional.

Before scientist or astronaut
Reached the universe
By flights or rockets
Poet reached the unimaginable distance
With their praiseworthy verses.
A poet is like a sketch of beauteous art
An engineer or scientist or astronaut
Are finishers of such thought.

So poet is fictional in his concept
Hence others are factual of the sort.

3. Rock

Rocks are the first ancient grant
of the God of the nature
Dated back to millions of years
As a friend gifted to you with a present
And opened it eagerly
Now human probe into rocks with technology .

We're crushing them wittingly or unwittingly
For the construction of buildings
Most of them thousands of years old
Present day business they're like gold
They're used for elegant floors
To beautify the internal structures .

Rocks are staunch pillars of earth grace
As any of the rock at our birthplace
Whenever we pass by its location
Feels like a kind of dedication
First we recognise the rocks
They're perennial and stable after storms.

Rock stones used to build everything
Caves as the human dwelling
For many prehistoric, neolithic or others

They're testament of past cultures
Ancient stone cities, temples, structures,
Stone tools of arrowheads
and from simple choppers to complex.

From humble shelters to monuments
Rock arts, cave paintings
Pyramids of Giza to Aihole and Pattadakal
Stone temples
Trees may last for thousand years
But rocks last from millennia to millions of years.

4.   Home

A home should be cozy with greens
Adjoining by lawns, floral trees
Two mango trees on the facade for ambiance
A home with ventilation through the doors and
windows
Inflow and outflow of air creates a healthy home.

A home is not just house or residence
A pack of family members
It's a place of big heart
Than any luxurious hotel or resort
A home is more than that
A sense of feeling with family
Every member has an intimacy
It's a flawless comfort zone with embrace.

If anyone progresses in the family
All wishes him cordially
If any event is there
Every member in family likes to celebrate
If there's a trauma to anyone
All members try to help him
With empathy as a member of union.

Earlier joint families enjoyed the delightful
vibrations
Now homes are with nuclear family trends
Hybrid families are in understanding blends
A home is a family mixed with
Feelings of sentiments and beliefs
A home with family members
Bonded with hearts and souls
An ultimate calm and peace of common source.

5. The Train

Many generations passed journeying by train
Who were fortunate of earlier days
Cheered such beautiful feeling of memory lanes
Whole world is indebted to the inventor of railways
Reminiscent the days whenever hearing the sound of
train
Wonderful past adventures of day and night

Yet, present day trains are luxurious and fast
Now, previous generations are missing the past
Unfortunately present era has no option left
Many cowboy movies were pictured
Watching whoever missed
Directly or Indirectly can be cherished .

Pleasant puffing sound of train
Passengers alluring through the window gazing nights
Looking intently sparkling fireflies .

Relishing rhythm of a train running over bridges
Captivating scene of huge snaky curve
Smokey train farther is yet to arrive
Passing through the long canyon
All along the golden sunshine.

6. Tiny bird

As I stepped on the road
I stared at the trees,
In a relaxed way I heard a bird's voice ,
From thick green bushes
I stared in the lush green leaves ,
But the bird stopped its whistle,,
After a while I started walking slowly ,
As I heard birds tweet frequently ,
Wherever greenery is there ,
I started stepping further ,
Once again I listened to the chirping of tiny bird,
As if inviting me with its whistle
And its tweet is only for me,
Now an interest evoked me,
To watch the little bird
Since last three days, whenever
I pass by the route leisurely ,
Same bird chirruped I heard recurrently ,
Once more I looked into the bushes to inquire eagerly ,
I could hear twittering repeatedly ,
I gazed at small hummingbird
tuneful voice persistently ,
I love its lively chirping sound ,
Amazed to watch such a small bird,

With its lovely little bird ways
After few moments the bird flew away ,
From tilting tiny branches as I stared .

7. Wheels

Wheels have marked a revolution
In the dawn of global transportation
Similarly epitomised in trade transition
Right from the invention of wooden wheel
In ancient era were used for the transit. .
The copper and iron wheels introduced
Stage after stage, efficiently evolved .

Anyway a wheel is a wheel
Big wheels with rims
The mini wheels of bearings
Which's the core of a giant wheel
Or for rotating cylindrical fields

The transit of wheels changed global trade
Whether small or big sprocket and gear
Acceleration of human life by variable machineries
To enhance the transit efficiencies

Wooden wheels and then copper wheels
Used in three thousand two hundred BCE
For transport purpose of copper mines
And for the fast industrial growth lines.

Conclusively, a wheel is a wheel
Whether steel or copper or rubber radial
Used for planes, buses, cars, trains, rovers on Mars
A drastic transit form invented wooden wheel carts.

.

8. Forest

Our planet is bestowed by green belt
Most of them enveloped in the form of forest
Forests are lungs of the earth
Like humans need oxygen to breath
Amazing Amazon forest with variant plants
Produce most of the oxygen by any other on land.

Once entered into the forest
Everything unknowingly we forget
Walking along the narrow path
May lead to mini ponds
Swimming and diving of big and small animals
Or may take to some other
access to further tall trees..

While hearing the sounds of monkeys
Twitters of birds and sounds of flies
All those audible sounds reflects
Each other invisible creatures
All over the site
Animals foot impressions
Seldom on marshy place .

Forests are treasures of the nature

Filled with fauna and flora
with animals birds
and plants of assorted
All are big treasures of the earth.

9. Floret

As I went out on a countryside
For a leisurely walk in the dusk
My eyes fallen on an area of mire
On a solo plant in the muck
With a engrossing floret
In purple impel me to stare at.

I was wondered and startled to know
How come on sludge its grown
My pensive thoughts arouse
As a ravishing flower from a sludge
Like gold and silver too from the mines
Beneath the surface of the earth
Pretty floral plants can grow from the mires.

After all the beauty is created from the soil
So also this solo plant is from muck and slime

Next day as I was walking that side
And looking at the plant when I am passing by
Instantly reacting to the drizzle
Flower is slightly swaying
With glossy leaves dancing
Like a kid enjoy the showers

In the rhythm of the flower

Leaves are swinging in the showers.

10. Supreme Power

If anyone says
Is there a God in this world?
I say yes, its an absolute supreme power

But can be prayed in an atmosphere
For spiritual, social ,
and psychological reasons
Providing a sacred place for rituals
Churches, mosques and temples
Which are created for
peace of mind by ancestors .

The God is not just in,Churches
Mosques and Temples
In the form of worshipping places
For divinity and devotion
Worship the God with gratitude and appreciation

All Epics are to follow the good
And leave the bad to avoid
Epics are just an eye openers
To drive away the evil powers
Just don't pray for desires
But to eradicate trouble and pains

and instead strive for those requires .

A misconception of sentiment is there
If visiting disciples are more
Power of a church, temple God will grow
If power is more, more disciples wish to see the God.

The God is a belief
Not just sentiment
Worship any stone
From heart and soul
You can feel impactful .

Pray from heart and soul
With good intentions for ourselves
and who're helpless
But not bad intention on others.

11. Everlasting

Dawn of the moon
An everlasting nature boon
Seems as if rising from the ocean
Changing black water into blue .
As the silky waves turns to
All along the orange rays .
Appears to be spreading silky orange surface
Curling rays on one another
Gradual raising heights together .
Moon fascinated by the ocean water
Can be seen obviously as validated
Every moment I walked so delighted .
The coloured silky cloth furls and unfurls
Concurrent of wave curls
As the moment of wondrous unfurls
And curls recalls my-love lovely engross.
Few minutes, I couldn't resist myself from emotions
The feelings of glowing moments .
Lasted for few minutes
Till the orange rays turned to silver
Though the waves consistently raising
As the moon gently rising .

12. Mom

Without any dearth
Mom's care and control
Right from the birth
A kid as parents soul
Grown up teen in faith.

Engulfed in plans and hope
As the schooling advances
Mind plays a big role
Journey of man commences
Ensure to unlock the source.

Longing for bright future
An opportunity for golden gate
As predicts in self favour
A pivotal of one's fate
Leading light of the stature.

13. Depression

Depression can be a curse
When you are in solitude even worsen
People may say you do this, you do that
For relief it depends on your mindset

As it's mostly connected to mind and heart .
You have to seek your own relief to come out
Of what you are feeling deep inside
Which may lead to tedious often times .

One must go to the root cause
Of the situation for solipsism
You are reluctant to any happiness
Once you are exited from the moment of locus .

You would feel more cheerful and winsome
As you have a great escape from the hell of depression
As you are blessed with savvy vision.

14. Scenic

As flow of thoughts awaken my insights
To write what it whispers in the midnight
Saying 'catch me up as I may disappear,'
Before that put pen to paper
On behalf of you in public favour .

It says many things about nature
Of a lake with a charming scene
Encompassing by willow trees
A mid of the ridges variant species
Of birds resting view, flew off few.

Blue sky reflecting on water
as crystal clear scattered
During the fall, fall off trees
Aroused me with scented breeze.

A lovely euco pink wilted leaves
Spinning gently from the heights
An appealing moment of gazing
eyes.
Touching the ground in slow tempo
Juncture of decorative gusto
Swinging all boughs at one side

Like up and down in rhythmic style
Shining silver waters of the lake.

Bordered with the ridges safe
In graceful sun rays
On my way in midday
In the middle of the waterways
My eyes watching through says,
The bushes sparkling sun rays
While I was travelling by the boat
My thoughts filled with delight
As to quite as per my insight .

15. Guilty heart

The tongue and throat
Can threaten or deceit
Anyone with his loud tone
Express by hiding facts
Which later on reacts
Whoever maybe with astute
However he may be smart
Can't deceive his own heart
Have a glance over the sky
Covered with dark cloud
Flying birds passing by
Sounds of thunders loud and loud
One can't predict a bright sunshine
But a plausible pelting rain
The rain ceased
As the cloud passes away
The betrayed lies ended
As again sun groomed the day
Birds flying high and high
The sun cleared the sky.

16. Cell Phone

Earlier for passion or status
Now like a partner of insistence
Prolonged buzz rattling and shaking
Ring , Ring and Birring
A cell phone's persistent buzzing .
Seldom received sad or wrong calls
At times happy and joyous calls
Leads to go to shopping malls
Or to attend convention halls
Apart from the crazy calls .
Cell phone is not just
A phone for calls, but
Its an excellent media
Of any global area
Small piece dominated TVs and cinemas
Videos and cameras,
At the outset, for business people
As an expensive piece
To save the time and fuel
Now compulsion and affordable for all
In every one's hand playful .
Cell phones enabled us busy bee
Even though you're sick
You like to stick to it.

Cell phone had an elephant memory
Some of us maintain two regularly .
Manage password and WiFi
Once you get clarified
Accessible to social media
For an information and an idea.
Google, Facebook, Twitter, Instagram, WhatsApp etc.,
It covers twenty four hours news
Global voices and views .
A cell phone is not just a phone
A handy device like a magic box
Which has many incredible features
If you want, you can lock unlock.

17. Whispering

Who is this whispering me all the time
Who is this with mumbling lines
Sometimes my thinking refrained
Before sleeping distracting me every night
Now to show the way to enlighten
Who's that coming to my dreams to focus a light
Decade ago my love was futile
New hopes living as refit ship as usual to sail.
Who's that tattling me again ,
Please keep aloof, its my time ,
don't come again
My love is with me to enshrine
I pulled myself together to retain
As a repaired ship as usual back to life to sail.

18. Mirror

It will show you what you are
You may not accept what you saw
But mirror has the same display
You only move from side
to side ways
Watching it for twice or thrice
Yet, you are not satisfied
You need to compramise
Reflection is the same,
Image is the same
But you assume more glamour than what you are
This is a regular practice of human .
You can see this more and more
When watching mirror alone
Instantly your image never changes .
But your eyes and mind
perceives image
Then you saw eye to eye
With the mirror
Then you say , yes,
It's my error,
Iam not that beauteous,
Than yester years,
So, I am getting old,

Witnessed my skin folds.
This is the feature
Of the every youth future.

19. Ocean

When we think of elated emotions
The breeze, dawn and dusk of the oceans
By the authors of the oceanic evocative atmosphere
Which ancient and current authors are inspired .

Gravitational force of the moon
was scientifically proven
That attracts the ocean
The known factors of present day notions
But the poets had an embraced
opinion of moon and ocean
Right from the ancient era they wrote
Countless love stories are in vogue
comparing with moon and ocean .

Oceans are ancient ships pride
Sailing to long distance even in tides
Only source of large scale trades
From continent to continent by waves
Which left many impressions by pirates
Lost treasures left beneath the surface.

Sailing is a pleasant journey currently
For sea sickness we have good remedy

As we can't resist the pleasure of breeze
Oceans are for global certainties.

20. Artist

Lacking its finishing touch
The best art work of a man
Unsatisfied at times to such
Wondrous artistic paragon.

Like, last puff of a cigarette
Which makes to think again
Missing something paramount
As last sip of a wine.

With preoccupied mind
Couldn't get, but tried
Come what may by a side
But baffled and dissatisfied.

Resumes for final touch up
Could see exterior variation
Finally he made up
With full gratification.

21. Music

Anyone can freely try
Different world of joy
As you enjoy the tasty delicious dish
In music whatever melodies you wish
Like you enjoy every bite of dish
Every bit of music you relish .

It has multilingual power
And can unite all in fervour
Music has varied facets
With different rhythmic modes
Can create millions of songs
With multifarious tunings
Can create soulful timings.

Music is the universal language
Music is not just a language,
It has omnipresent feeling,
Power of uniting all cast and creed .

We visit divine places for piece of mind in calm and
composed
In concerts to stimulate mind and heart with sweet
music compose .

Divine places for enlightenment with devoted silence
Concert places filled with musical entertainment in the
light of synchronise.

But the God is supreme invincible and invisible
Music can lit the divine spark connected to spiritual
With divine power which is audible and visible .
In music everyone has a different taste
They have their own choice to play .
Listening music is an art
Melodic music compose is nice craft.

Philosophers say music can heal the patients
All sounds lead to music ocean.

www.ingramcontent.com/pod-product-compliance
Lightning Source LLC
Chambersburg PA
CBHW050953030426
42339CB00007B/379